**How do you know when Dracula catches a virus?**

*He's always coffin.*

**Why do they call it the Novel Virus?**

*It's a long story.*

D1522626

**You want to hear a hilarious joke about the new virus?**

*You probably wouldn't get it.*

**COMPILED BY JOHN CONRAD**

Because of regulations, I had to
omit the actual name of the virus
causing the current
pandemic in 2020, when
publishing this book.

Feel free to use the
actual name of the
virus when reading jokes from
this book.

Simply substitute the word
"virus" with the actual name.

Thank you for understanding.

**How is the news about this new virus like a photographer?**

*It won't stop developing.*

**The amount of bad virus jokes is starting to reach worrying numbers...**

*Some scientists claim it might become a pundemic.*

**Before the virus, I used to cough to hide a fart...**

*Now I fart to hide a cough.*

**Did you hear that cows can give you the virus?**

*It's fake moos.*

**Because of this pandemic, did you know that people have been buying more toilet paper than ever before?**

*If this keeps up we'll be wiped out!*

**Why did everyone on the cruise get infected with the virus?**

*They were all in the same boat.*

**I could tell jokes about the virus...**

*But Achoos not to.*

**Did you know that scientists are working on a vaccine for the virus?**

*I think it's worth a shot.*

**Some people aren't shaking hands because of the virus...**

*I'm not shaking hands because everyone is out of toilet paper.*

**What do you call teenagers with this virus?**

*Quaranteens.*

**Why are my mom's sisters immune to all viruses?**

*It's because of their aunt-ey bodies.*

**Do you know why we shouldn't tell any more virus pandemic jokes?**

*People are getting sick of them.*

**What are the most popular jokes during quarantine?**

*Inside jokes.*

**Do you know why my mirror is really enjoying quarantine?**

*It has a lot time to reflect.*

**Why did a woman stop making a belt out of watches during quarantine?**

*It was a waist of time.*

**Why was the man quarantined after he I tried to put icing on a cake?**

*He wanted to prevent risk of spreading confection.*

**Why were the passengers on the airplane quarantined after the flight?**

*They all flu together.*

**I ran out of toilet paper, so have begun using old newspapers...**

Times are rough.

**Still no toilet paper at the store today...**

*My dad said they're wiped out.*

**What's the human psychology behind all this toilet paper hoarding?**

*That's just how we roll.*

**What's the max amount of toilet paper you can have?**

*A butt load.*

**Why aren't there more dad jokes about toilet paper?**

*Because they're tear-able.*

**Did you hear about the new government advice about using lettuce leaves if you have no toilet paper?**

*It's the tip of the iceberg.*

**Do you know why we bought extra toilet paper for the quarantine party?**

*It's for the party poopers.*

**What has toilet paper become?**

*A precious commode-ity.*

**Do you know what might happen if we run out of toilet paper due to this crisis?**

*Using newspaper might be the new headline.*

**I went to the store and they were out of toilet paper....**

*All we have left at the house is sandpaper. Things are getting rough.*

**Why couldn't the toilet paper cross the road?**

*It got stuck in a crack.*

**Do you want to come to my quarantine party?**

*B.Y.O.R (Bring Your Own Roll)*

**Did you know there's no toilet paper anywhere in my town?**

*Guess you could say there's been a massive run on it.*

**People are selling toilet paper for how much?!**

*I've just been flushing it down the toilet.*

**Where does toilet paper come from?**

*Toiletries.*

**Why did the toilet paper roll down the hill?**

*To get to the bottom.*

**What's a mathematician's favorite type of toilet paper?**

*Multiply.*

**Did you know that toilet paper is more dangerous than the virus itself?**

*It wipes out millions of people every day.*

**Why is toilet paper shy?**

*It gets flushed easily.*

**Why do toilet paper rolls have trust issues?**

*They're always getting ripped off.*

**How do you bake toilet paper?**

*I'm not really sure, but I know how to brown it on one side.*

**Why are toilet paper salesmen were born to succeed?**

*They were meant to ply their trade.*

**Do you know why my job at the toilet paper company really stinks?**

All they care about is the bottom line.

**Everyone talks about how good their brand of toilet paper is...**

*But in my experience, they are all pretty crappy after I use them.*

**What do toilet paper and numbers have in common?**

*Both can be multi-ply'd!*

**What did Shakespeare say when buying toilet paper?**

*2-ply or not 2-ply. That is the question.*

**Why shouldn't you get in a price war over toilet paper?**

*Because no matter what, it's a race to the bottom.*

**I got in touch with my inner-self today.**

*That's the last time I use cheap toilet paper.*

**What do you use to wipe... your left or right hand?**

*I just use toilet paper.*

**Why are virus jokes are the funniest...**

*Because everyone gets it.*

**This virus pandemic has caused my local shop to start stocking dead batteries...**

*Because they're free of charge!*

**Want to hear a funny virus joke?**

*Nevermind, you probably won't get it.*

**I tried to come up with a joke about social distancing...**

*This is as close as I could get...*

**Did you hear that garlic helps to prevent virus?**

*People will automatically social distance from you.*

**What do you call a person who doesn't believe in the virus?**

A COVidiot

**Why do a lot of people get virus jokes?**

*Because they are really infectious.*

**Quarantine has allowed me time to start a boat building business in my garage.**

*So far, sails are through the roof!*

**Did you know that all countries finally got the virus?**

*China got it right off the bat.*

**Why should mailmen go onto quarantine right away?**

*They're really good carriers.*

**Why is this new virus so popular?**

*It really went viral.*

**Why aren't there many people infected by the virus in Antarctica?**

*Because they're so ice-olated.*

**Why don't chefs find virus jokes funny?**

*They are in bad taste.*

**Why are people hoarding all the toilet paper?**

*Because the virus is scaring the crap out of everybody.*

## MORE DAD JOKES...

**How do you throw birthday party in outer space?**

*You planet.*

**Did you hear about the lady who lost the right side of her body?**

*She's allright now.*

**Why was the raccoon lying in the middle of the street?**

*He got tired.*

**Why don't they don't allow gambling during a safari?**

*Too many Cheetahs.*

**Why don't we switch from pounds to kilograms overnight?**

*Because there would be mass confusion.*

**Want to hear a joke about a piece of paper?**

*Nevermind, it's tearable.*

**Did you hear about the restaurant on mars?**

*Great food but the atmosphere is horrible.*

**How many cherries grow on a cherry tree?**

*All of them.*

**How does an eskimo build a house?**

*Igloos it together.*

**Why did the goldfish think they were fighting a war?**

*They were inside a tank.*

**What is the name of a man with no legs and no arms in a swimming pool?**

*Bob*

**What is the name of a man who can't stand?**

*Neil*

**Have you heard of the band called 678 megabytes?**

*If you haven't, that's okay, they haven't had a gig yet.*

**Why did the rooster cross the road?**

*To prove it wasn't a chicken.*

**Why did the golfer wear two pairs of pants?**

*In case he got a hole in one.*

**What did the mother horse say to the baby horse?**

*It's past-ure bedtime.*

**What do you call a horse that lives in the house next to you?**

*A neeeeeeigh-bor.*

**Why isn't the english teacher friends with every single letter of the alphabet?**

*She doesn't know 'Y.'*

**Why can't a mountain bike stand on it's own?**

*It's two tired.*

**What happened when the brunette got her hair bleached?**

*She got light-headed.*

**What did the ocean do when it saw the beach?**

*It waved.*

**What does a watch do when it's hungry?**

*It goes back for seconds.*

**Why can't towels and wash rags tell jokes?**

*They have a dry sense of humor.*

**What do you call a cow who can't stand up straight?**

*Lean beef.*

**What do you call a cow without it's legs?**

*Ground beef.*

**Why did the teacher become crosseyed?**

*He could't control his pupils.*

**Why did the clown retire after a bad juggling accident?**

*He didn't have the balls to do it anymore.*

**Why isn't the runner afraid of hurdles anymore?**

*He got over it.*

**Why didn't the hyena win the race?**

*It was racing a cheetah.*

**Why did the tomatoe turn red?**

*Because it saw the salad dressing.*

**Why don't vampires eat meat?**

*They don't like steaks.*

**Why did the poster go to jail even though it was innocent?**

*It was framed.*

**What do you call a bear with no teeth?**

*A gummy bear.*

**Did you know they finally made a movie about clocks?**

*It's about time.*

**How do you know someone isn't addicted to brake fluid?**

*They can stop whenever they want.*

**What should you do if you have a fear of elevators?**

*Take steps to avoid them.*

**What did the buffalo say to his son when he left?**

*Bison*

**Why can't you trust elevators?**

*They're always up to something*

.

**Why did the Energizer bunny get arrested?**

*It was charged with battery.*

**Why did the skeleton go to the movie along?**

*He didn't have any-body to go with.*

**Why didn't the skeleton ask the lady on a date?**

*He didn't have any guts.*

**How did the lady feel when metal objects stopped shocking her when she touched them?**

*Ec-static.*

**Why did the muffler stop working?**

*It was exhausted.*

**Did you hear about the circus fire?**

*It was in-tents.*

**Why did a hiker pack a phone?**

*In case nature called.*

**Why was the father called a hero when he wouldn't let his son sleep in the middle of the day?**

*He prevented a kidnapping.*

**Which language in the world is spoken less than any other?**

*Sign language*

**Did you hear about the nacho joke?**

*Nevermind, it's too cheesy.*

**Why can't you trust atoms?**

*They make up everything.*

**Did you hear about the dinosaur hiphop artist?**

*He was a famous raptor.*

**Why did the astronaut break up with his girlfriend?**

*He needed some space.*

**What do you give a sick bird?**

*Tweetment*

**Why don't oysters share it's belongings?**

*Because their shellfish.*

**What do you call fake noodles?**

*Impastas!*

**Why was the rasberry crying?**

*Because it's friends were in a jam.*

**How do chickens get someone to do something for them?**

*They egg them on.*

**What do you call a belt with a watch on it?**

*A waist of time.*

**Why shouldn't you sketch with a broken drawing pencil?**

*It's pointless.*

**What do you call a bear when there is not one bee is around?**

*Ears.*

**What did the judge say when someone farted?**

*Odor in the court!*

**How do you defend yourself from a queen bee?**

*With a B B gun.*

**Did you hear about the 4 thiefs that stole a calendar?**

*They each got 3 months.*

**What did the tomato say to the hot dog?**

*I'll catchup to you.*

**What do you call food that isn't yours?**

Nachos!

**Why did the traffic lights turn red?**

*It changed in the middle of the intersection.*

**What did the blanket say when the maid ripped it off the bed?**

*I thought you had me covered.*

**Why didn't the lifeguard save the drowning hippy?**

*He was too far out man!*

**Why did a baker open a bakery?**

*To make some dough.*

**What do you call a rattlesnake who can't rattle?**

*A reptile dysfunction.*

**How many people live in Brazil?**

*A brazilian.*

**How do you know you were attacked by a vampire snowman?**

*You have frostbite.*

**What happened when a frog parked his car illegally?**

*It got toad.*

**What do you call a person who never farts in public?**

*A private tutor.*

**What is a vampires favorite drink?**

*A bloody mary.*

**What is a vampire's favorite dog?**

*A blood hound.*

**Why did the science teacher stop telling jokes in class?**

*He didn't get a reaction.*

**Why did the cookie cry?**

*Because his father was a wafer so long!*

**Why should you never go to a seafood disco?**

*You could pull a mussel.*

**Do you know where you can get chicken broth in bulk?**

*The stock market.*

**Why did the octopus beat the shark in a fight?**

*Because it was well armed.*

**How much does a hipster weigh?**

*An instagram.*

**What did daddy spider say to baby spider?**

*You spend too much time on the web.*

**What is atheism?**

*It's a non-prophet organization.*

**Did you hear about the brand new broom they invented?**

*It's sweeping the nation.*

**What cheese can never be yours?**

Nacho cheese.

**What did the Buffalo say to his little boy when he dropped him off at school?**

*Bison.*

**Have you ever heard of a music group called Cellophane?**

*They mostly wrap.*

**How was Rome split in two?**

*With a pair of Ceasars.*

**What is a shovel?**

*It's a ground breaking invention.*

**What did the Buddhist say when it walked up to a hot dog stand?**

*Make me one with everything.*

**What do you call a girl with one leg that's shorter than the other?**

*Ilene.*

**Did you hear about the theatrical performance about puns?**

*It was a play on words.*

**Do you know sign language?**

*You should learn it, it's pretty handy.*

**Why was one banana attracted to the other?**

*Because she was appealing.*

**Did you read the book about antigravity?**

*I couldn't put it down.*

**What should you do if you are cold?**

*Stand in the corner. It's 90 degrees.*

**How does Moses make coffee?**

*Hebrews it.*

**What did the alien say to the pitcher of water?**

*Take me to your liter.*

**Did you hear about the soldier who survived mustard gas and pepper spray?**

*He was a seasoned veteran.*

**Did you read the book about glue?**

*I couldn't put it down.*

**Why shouldn't you trust atoms?**

*They make up everything.*

**What's it called when you have too many aliens?**

*Extraterrestrials.*

**What do cows tell each other at bedtime?**

*Dairy tales.*

**Why didn't the lion win the race?**

*Because he was racing a cheetah.*

**What's it called when you put a cow in a hot air balloon?**

*Raising the steaks.*

**Why don't vampires go to barbecues?**

*They don't like steaks.*

**How do trees access the internet?**

*They log on.*

**Why should you never trust a train?**

*They have loco motives.*

**Did you see the ad for burial plots in todays newspaper? It's the last thing**

*I need.*

**Have you ever tried fixing a clock?**

*It's very time consuming.*

**Why can't bicycles stand up on their own?**

*They are 2 tired.*

**What would happen if the alarm clocks hit you back in the morning?**

*It would be truly alarming.*

**Why is a skeleton a bad liar?**

*You can see right through it.*

**What do you receive when you ask a lemon for help?**

*Lemonaid.*

Made in the USA
Monee, IL
27 May 2021

69679493R00035